BUSES IN SOUTH AND WEST YORKSHIRE

PETER TUCKER

This book is dedicated to Tabitha.

Front cover above: First No. 37112 passes through industrial Brightside, Sheffield, bound for Doncaster on 10 September 2021.

Front cover below: First No. 69571, pictured at work in Laisterdyke, Bradford, bound for Tyersal.

Back cover: Heavy traffic provides a challenge for First Leeds buses at Harehills on 5 November 2021.

First published 2023

Amberley Publishing
The Hill, Stroud
Gloucestershire, GL5 4EP

www.amberley-books.com

Copyright © Peter Tucker, 2023

The right of Peter Tucker to be identified as the Author of this work has been asserted in accordance with the Copyrights, Designs and Patents Act 1988.

ISBN 978 1 3981 1407 4 (print)
ISBN 978 1 3981 1408 1 (ebook)

All rights reserved. No part of this book may be reprinted or reproduced or utilised in any form or by any electronic, mechanical or other means, now known or hereafter invented, including photocopying and recording, or in any information storage or retrieval system, without the permission in writing from the Publishers.

British Library Cataloguing in Publication Data.
A catalogue record for this book is available from the British Library.

Origination by Amberley Publishing.
Printed in the UK.

Introduction

Buses in South and West Yorkshire is a photographic survey of the current bus scene in the aforementioned counties. The aim of this book is simple: to show buses at work in a variety of contrasting environments; from large cities such as Sheffield, to the more suburban or rural parts of metropolitan Yorkshire such as Addingham, Herdings, Horsforth, Tickhill and Warmsworth. A few photographs from the 1990s have also been included as a nostalgic touch.

The former metropolitan counties of South and West Yorkshire were formed in April 1974 as a result of the Local Government Act 1972. These new counties brought the heavily populated parts of Yorkshire together in supposedly stronger units. The more rural areas of Yorkshire became the new counties of North Yorkshire and Humberside. Parts of the old West Riding went to Cumbria, Lancashire and Greater Manchester. Parts of the East Riding, such as Riccall, went to North Yorkshire, together with most of the rural West Riding including Harrogate, High Bentham, Ripon, Selby, and Settle. Goole went over to Humberside, in the now largely forgotten Boothferry district.

South Yorkshire PTE (Passenger Transport Executive) and West Yorkshire PTE were responsible for the provision and coordination of public transport in their domains. The former was notable for having a notoriously expensive low-fare policy for users of public transport. Apart from Barnsley district, South Yorkshire PTE was the dominant operator in the county. West Yorkshire PTE was based in Wakefield, a district where it had a limited presence due to the dominance of the National Bus Company. In the 1980s NBC buses within West Yorkshire, such as Yorkshire Woollen, were required to use the PTE's Verona green livery, plus 'Metro' branding. The PTE was abolished in 2014 and is now known as the West Yorkshire Combined Authority. The 'Metro' branding remains in use.

Deregulation and the abolition of the metropolitan counties in 1986 led to the sell-off of the PTE-operated bus companies. South Yorkshire PTE eventually became Mainline, and is today First South Yorkshire. In fact, as this introduction was being written, First South Yorkshire was being split into new divisions based on Doncaster, Rotherham and Sheffield. New liveries were also being adopted as will be seen in the photographic section.

West Yorkshire PTE became Yorkshire Rider, and is today First West Yorkshire. At the time of writing, the West Yorkshire divisions were First Bradford, First Calderdale & Huddersfield, and First Leeds. Both counties had National Bus Company subsidiaries including West Riding – Yorkshire, West Yorkshire Road Car and Yorkshire Traction. The remains of these companies are now owned by Arriva, First, Stagecoach and Transdev respectively. Apart from some heritage liveries and surviving depots, all traces of these companies have vanished.

The independent bus companies have largely disappeared – Black Prince, Felix, Leon, and Premier et al – together with most of those created after deregulation. The likes of Yorkshire Terrier were absorbed by Yorkshire Traction, who subsequently sold-out to

Stagecoach in 2005. Keighley & District, which was carved out of West Yorkshire Road Car in 1987, is now part of Transdev. The company started under AJS auspices in 1987, before passing to Blazefield in 1991. Transdev acquired Blazefield in 2006 and continues to pursue imaginative marketing schemes today.

West Yorkshire Metropolitan County was created in 1974 and abolished in 1986. The five constituent boroughs of West Yorkshire are Bradford, Calderdale, Leeds, Kirklees and Wakefield. Today, the combined population of West Yorkshire is estimated to be about 2.3 million with the Bradford area having a notably youthful and diverse population. The largest district in West Yorkshire is Leeds, the commercial powerhouse of the entire region. Blessed by excellent communications and a broad economic base, Leeds has suffered fewer urban problems than some other northern conurbations such as Manchester. Apart from the eponymous city, the district includes a variety of market and industrial towns including Garforth, Morley, Pudsey, Otley, Rothwell and Wetherby. The north of the district includes affluent villages including Boston Spa, Bramhope, Collingham, Harewood and Pool. There is moorland at Hawksworth, and a string of small, suburbanised towns based around Guiseley, Horsforth and Yeadon. The south of the district is more industrial in character and includes former mining communities including Allerton Bywater, Methley and Micklefield. The principal bus operators in Leeds today are First and Arriva.

To the west of Leeds is Bradford Metropolitan District. Bradford is the chief settlement, followed by Keighley. Much of the district is characterised by Victorian architecture, steep hills, and the remnants of the textile industries. Mills are still a prominent feature in the area. the Manningham Mills feature a 250-foot-tall chimney, visible around much of Bradford.

Bradford is well known for waves of immigration, the Pakistani community being the most prominent. Large areas of Bradford including Bradford Moor, Girlington, Little Horton, Manningham and Thornbury have a strongly Asian atmosphere in contrast to Baildon, Queensbury and Wyke.

Bradford district has numerous other settlements including the inland resort of Ilkley, and villages popular with tourists – Esholt, Haworth and Oxenhope. The towns of Baildon, Bingley, Queensbury, Silsden and Shipley are popular with commuters who work in Bradford, Halifax and Leeds. The dominant bus operator in Bradford today is First, while Transdev, operating in various colours, are the principal operator in the Keighley area.

Calderdale's landscape is a dramatic mixture of hills, mills and moors. The historic town of Halifax is the chief settlement in the district. The town is bounded by steeply banked hills giving the impression of being in a large bowl. Although the town can appear bleak on a wet day, the town has many architectural merits including Piece Hall (1775) and Wainhouse Tower (1875). Akroyden and Copley are planned industrial suburbs, less well known than Saltaire in Bradford. The other towns in Calderdale are all interesting, and include Brighouse, Elland, Hebden Bridge, Ripponden and Todmorden, which are all served principally by First or Team Pennine.

Like Calderdale, Kirklees is not named after any town in the district. The name is derived from Kirklees Priory, which is actually in Calderdale. Huddersfield is the dominant town of Kirklees. Vastly underrated, Huddersfield has some impressive streets and one of the best railway stations in Yorkshire. Pritchett's classical station, constructed between 1847 and 1848, is a fantastic point of entry, or exit, to the town. Huddersfield has a diverse population, with well over 20 per cent of residents coming from a visible minority. The other key urban area of Kirklees is centred on Spenborough, Batley and Dewsbury. Generally known as the 'Heavy Woollen District', various villages and towns combine to form a compact and distinctive industrial area sandwiched between Bradford, Huddersfield, Leeds and Wakefield. Batley and Dewsbury have a very significant Asian population with many mosques and continental food stores.

The other parts of Kirklees are more rural in character and include Holmfirth, Marsden and Meltham, towards the Peak District National Park. Near Denby Dale are a string of lesser-known settlements including Clayton West, Emley and Upper Cumberworth. The main bus operators in Kirklees are First, Arriva and Team Pennine.

Wakefield district is based around the eponymous city, and includes the historic town of Pontefract. Wakefield is a town of some history and was once more important than Bradford or Leeds. Large industrial estates have replaced the mining and textile interests of the district. Other towns in the wider district include Castleford, Hemsworth and Ossett. There are several former mining communities including Featherstone, Normanton and South Elmsall, plus numerous pretty villages such as Ackworth, Wentbridge and Wooley. One of the districts most interesting places is Heath Common, an unexpected oasis just minutes from Wakefield, and once dominated by a now demolished power station. Newmillerdam, off Barnsley Road, comes a close second.

South Yorkshire Metropolitan County was once known, unofficially, as the Socialist Republic of South Yorkshire. Formed mainly from the old West Riding, the county also included parts of Derbyshire and Nottinghamshire. South Yorkshire's unitary boroughs are Barnsley, Doncaster, Rotherham and Sheffield. The population of South Yorkshire is about 1.405 million.

Barnsley district is built upon coal, and traces of the industry are visible for those with good eyes, a map and a vivid imagination. Many of South Yorkshire's mining sites have been totally obliterated. Cortonwood at Rotherham is now a leisure park; its threatened closure triggered the 1984 miners' strike. Barnsley is an old town, which expanded rapidly in Victorian times. Much of the town was reconstructed in the 1960s and today it is being rebuilt again, and so far the designs do not look promising. Former colliery towns and villages comprise a significant portion of the district and include Dodworth, Grimethorpe, Hoyland, Royston, Thurnscoe, Wombwell, and so forth. Penistone has a more Pennine character, while lonely Dunford Bridge guards the disused Woodhead Tunnel amidst bleak moorland landscapes. The principal bus operator in Barnsley today is Stagecoach.

Rotherham is another old town that gives its name to a wider district. Steel made Rotherham prosperous and scarred much of the landscape around the River Don. The compact town centre includes the stately All Saints (in the Perpendicular style) and Bridge Chapel, plus a typically brutal post-war bus station. Low hills surround Rotherham in all directions, providing good prospects of the steel plants and the countryside towards Wentworth. The borough's other key settlements include Maltby, Rawmarsh, Swinton and Wath-upon-Dearne, all previously centres of heavy industry. There are several former colliery villages including Dinnington and Thurcroft, plus unexpectedly charming settlements such as Hooton Roberts, Ravenfield and Wentworth. Rotherham's architectural treasures include Wentworth Woodhouse, and the romantic remains of Roche Abbey, near Maltby. An interesting mix of the urban and semi-rural, Rotherham district deserves to be better known.

The district of Doncaster extends from the fringes of Rotherham and Barnsley to the flat landscape bordering the East Riding and Lincolnshire. The town of Doncaster dates back to at least Roman times, and was later a key point on the Great North Road. Railways and the local collieries helped the town prosper, but what remains today is an uneasy mix of old and new. From April 1974, Doncaster was expanded to include several contrasting settlements including Adwick-le-Street, Askern, Bawtry, Conisborough, Hatfield, Mexborough and Thorne. The ruined keep of Conisborough Castle is a spectacular monument to Norman power and an unexpected highlight of the Dearne Valley. Doncaster includes a wide variety of villages: Burghwallis, Fishlake, Hickleton, Moorends, Tickhill and Warmsworth. Finningley was previously in Nottinghamshire, and is now the location of the doomed Robin Hood (Doncaster Sheffield) Airport. A glance at any map reveals the fascinating street plan of New Rossington, which resembles a bicycle from above. There are similar circular patterns at Armthorpe and Woodlands. The principal provider of bus services today in Doncaster is First, with Stagecoach working in from Barnsley and Rotherham, plus Nottinghamshire.

Sheffield dominates South Yorkshire much more than Leeds does West Yorkshire. Chaucer referenced the city and Mary, Queen of Scots was held captive at the now demolished castle. Cutlery and steel built Sheffield's reputation. Extremely hilly, the city is characterised by a wide variety of post-war architecture. Notable social housing schemes, not all of them successful, include Park Hill, Woodside and Gleadless. Ostensibly urban, much of Sheffield is actually rural and includes a portion of the Peak District National Park (along with Barnsley and Kirklees). Sheffield includes the towns of Ecclesfield and Stocksbridge, plus lofty villages such as Ewden and Bradfield. The old parishes of Bradfield, Ecclesfield and Sheffield were once in an area known as Hallamshire, a name that can still be found in the city today. The principal bus operators in Sheffield today are First and Stagecoach.

I hope you enjoy this survey of the buses, towns and villages of South and West Yorkshire. I have attempted to include a wide variety of places, from Bawtry to Bradford, and a wide variety of bus types. This book is not a bus guide per se; those wanting to know more about buses and transport operators are recommended to explore the vast array of literature produced by the likes of British Bus Publishing, the PSV Circle, and other organisations or publications. The internet is also a valuable source of information for bus lovers. I would highly recommend the likes of 'Lost-Albion' by Kevin Lane on Flickr, for those who want to explore photographs of towns and transport from the recent past.

I would like to thank Thomas Anthony for proofreading the text, plus Miss Alice, Sister Margaret Atkins, Mary, and all at Amberley Publishing. All photographs are by the author. Finally, any errors in this book are mine.

Peter Tucker
Allithwaite, Cumbria

Severe-looking post-war architecture forms the background for Arriva No. 1711, in historic Pontefract, West Yorkshire, on 11 March 2022.

Otley is a market and mill town on the River Wharfe, almost, but not quite in North Yorkshire. More workaday than nearby Ilkley, Otley has plenty of character and dignified stone buildings, set under a steep ridge known as The Chevin. In July 1997, First Quickstep Travel, Dennis Dart/Alexander Dash No. 3241, pauses at traffic lights, amidst a typical Otley streetscape.

Yeadon was a key constituent in the Aireborough Urban District until its dissolution in 1974. Now part of Leeds, the name is still used to cover the area around Guiseley, Hawksworth and Rawdon. Transdev service 3 connects Bradford with Shipley, Guiseley, Leeds Bradford International Airport and Otley. Resplendent in 'Flyer' branding, Optare Versa No. 238 was seen in Town Street, Yeadon.

Horsforth claims to be the largest village in England. A former urban district, Horsforth was incorporated into Leeds in 1974. At the end of Town Street is The Green, location of Roe-bodied Leyland Atlantean No. 6427. New to London Country in 1980, it came via Sovereign in 1989. Yorkshire Television recorded a number of television programmes in Horsforth, including *The Beiderbecke Tapes*.

The Square Peg was a moderately funny Norman Wisdom film released in 1958. SquarePeg, on the other hand, are a bus company based at Whitehall Road, Leeds. At Finkhill, Horsforth, MX10DXW, a Dennis Enviro200, works the Horsforth Circular towards the Ring Road on 4 November 2021.

First No. 35273 is a Wright StreetDeck Gemini, carrying a tasteful two-tone green livery and 'The Headingley Line' branding. Service 6 is well patronised by students around Otley Road and Woodhouse Lane who attend the various universities in Leeds. No. 35273 was photographed in the north-west suburbs of Leeds at Tinshill Road, Tinshill bound for the city centre.

CT Plus Yorkshire of Holbeck operate several school routes around Leeds. Pictured near Ralph Thoresby High School, Holt Park is this Plaxton-bodied Volvo B7TL. It was new to Durham Travel Services (New Cross) in 2001 for use in London. The destination is set for Cardinal Heenan School in Meanwood. Holt Park, November 2021.

The Leeds Guided Busway opened along the A61 to much fanfare in 1995. Similar schemes followed at York Road and Selby Road, Leeds, and Manchester Road, Bradford, in 2001. In harsh November light, First No. 39225 works south at King Lane, Moortown, on service 7. Other Leeds services such as the 51 avoid the busway altogether.

The A61 guided busway avoids Harrogate Road, Chapel Allerton, taking the faster Scott Hall Road to Leeds. Working the flagship service 36 between Ripon and Leeds at Harrogate Road is Transdev No. 3618. A Volvo B5TL/Wright Eclipse Gemini 3, it is luxuriously equipped for a public service vehicle. Service 36 once reached Ripon, in the hands of more utilitarian Bristol VRs and Leyland Nationals operated by West Yorkshire Road Car and United. Chapel Allerton, 4 November 2021.

Working along the fringe of Chapeltown and Sheepscar, with the tower blocks of Little London as a backdrop, is YX21RYG. It is an Alexander Dennis Enviro200, owned by Leeds Teaching Hospitals and seen traversing Chapeltown during November 2021.

Evening rush hour at Eastgate, Leeds, during October 1997. Roe-bodied Leyland Atlantean No. 6208 collects passengers for Wetherby. Together with Boston Spa, Collingham and East Keswick, Wetherby forms part of West Yorkshire's 'millionaire belt' or 'Golden Triangle'.

When the Yorkshire Rider divisions were split into separate subsidiaries, the Leeds City Link division adopted this ghastly red, orange and yellow livery. Working out to Pudsey in harsh sunshine, No. 5512 is a 1987 Leyland Olympian with rare Optare bodywork. Bringing up the rear is Black Prince No. 91, a Scania BR112, with equally uncommon Marshall bodywork, new to Newport in 1981.

Contrasting bus technology in Leeds. First No. 68807, a Yutong E10, carries 'Leeds City Electric' branding, representing the trend towards environmentally friendly power. On the left, the rear of Volvo B7RLE No. 69334 represents the old order – diesel power with a 7,300cc engine. Leeds, December 2021.

Typical of the current bus scene in Leeds are these Wright StreetDecks in First's attractive 'Leeds City' two-tone green. The location is Boar Lane, Leeds, with Holy Trinity (1721–27) dominating the background. The square tower was added in 1839.

Carrying a distinctive but by bus advertising standards relatively restrained overall advert for Wakefield College is West Riding No. 531. It is a typical Leyland Olympian/ECW combination photographed at St Peter's Street, Quarry Hill, Leeds, during March 1995. The now demolished Quarry Hill flats were a notable landmark in this area of Leeds. Completed in 1941 and inspired by municipal developments in Berlin, Paris and Vienna, they were bulldozed by 1978.

Contrasting liveries at Harehills. First No. 32437 is heading to Bramley in typical First colours. Bringing up the rear, No. 37675 (1812) carries the timeless West Yorkshire Road Car heritage livery. West Yorkshire Road Car, based in Harrogate, was sold to AJS Group by the National Bus Company in 1987. West Yorkshire ceased trading in 1989 as the company was split into individual units including Keighley & District and Yorkshire Coastliner. Yorkshire Rider acquired the Bradford, Leeds and York operations and absorbed them into their main fleet.

A close up of No. 37675 (1812), as it traverses the Burmantofts district of Leeds. A racially mixed area of Leeds, the district is the home of the renowned St James's University Hospital.

Working up Lincoln Green Road amidst often brutal post-war redevelopment is First No. 35209. The destination is incorrectly set for Old Farnley. Rows and rows of terraced streets were swept away from this part of east Leeds, which included the Globe Match Works, Hope Foundry and Mount Mills.

The same bus as it negotiates the densely populated streets around Strathmore Drive, Harehills, bound for Oakwood. Leeds is famous for its back-to-back houses. Many survive in Harehills, Farsley, Pudsey and elsewhere. The last back-to-backs were constructed in Leeds as late as 1937. Harehills, 20 November 2021.

Service 5 is a circular connecting Leeds city centre with Richmond Hill, East End Park, Osmondthorpe and Halton Moor. First No. 66997, a Volvo B7RLE/Wright combination, brightens up an unsettled day at Halton Moor on 5 November 2021. Neville Hill Sidings at Osmondthorpe are located close to this location in east Leeds.

Gipton is a large housing estate east of Harehills, comprised of both low- and high-rise dwellings. Construction started in 1934 on 'garden suburb' lines. This was an attempt to provide more attractive housing estates for working-class residents in contrast to the grim back-to-backs and terraces of many industrial cities. At Foundry Approach, Wright StreetDeck No. 35611 works towards Seacroft on 20 November 2021.

The hilly topography of Gipton can be seen in this picture of Wright StreetDeck No. 35209 at Oak Tree Drive. The relative space of Gipton contrasts with the overcrowded streets around Harehills. Gipton, 20 November 2021.

Proclaiming 'zero emissions', First No. 38401 is a BYD ADL Enviro400EV, dedicated to the Stourton Park & Ride facility in south Leeds. The bus has a range of 160 miles on a single charge. A BYD iron-phosphate battery pack is used on this innovative bus. Stourton, November 2021.

Temple Green Park & Ride is the location of First No. 35280, a Wright StreetDeck Gemini 3. These buses are marred by their rather uncomfortable seats and front window pillars, which partially obstruct views for some passengers. Temple Green is located near the M1 and Temple Newsham Park in south-east Leeds. 2 December 2021.

Pictured at Church Street, Hunslet, is YY67HBL, an Alexander Dennis Enviro200 in service with Powells Bus Co. Ltd. Typical inner-city terrain, Hunslet grew rapidly as a result of the Industrial Revolution and was described in Asa Briggs classic *Victorian Cities* as 'meanly built, consisting of narrow and dirty lanes'. Most of old Hunslet has been swept away, but the church of St Mary the Virgin (1862–64) survives as a prominent landmark in south Leeds.

Wright StreetDeck No. 35626 works up Town Street, Farsley, on service 16 to Pudsey. The small town of Farsley lost its independence to Pudsey at midnight, 31 March 1937. The Borough of Pudsey was absorbed by Leeds in 1974. Farsley, November 2021.

Tyersal has a split personality; most of the settlement is administered by the City of Leeds, as it is an outlier of Pudsey. A smaller portion of Tyersal forms part of Bradford around the fringe of Laisterdyke and Thornbury. Leaving the Bradford boundary and about to enter Leeds district for the terminus at Tyersal is First No. 69576.

One of the lesser-known battles of the English Civil War was the Battle of Adwalton Moor on 30 June 1643. Royalists won the battle at Drighlington, which cost the lives of approximately 700 soldiers. Squeezing between a Nissan Qashqai and a DAF CF, Arriva No. 1902 works towards Morley and Wakefield. Drighlington, February 2022.

The A639 connects Leeds with Castleford, Pontefract and ultimately Barnsdale Bar, north of Doncaster. Now less important as a corridor with the improvements to the A1M and M1, the road is nevertheless busy. On 20 November 2021, Arriva No. 1473 approaches Oulton, a desirable village just outside Rothwell.

Leaving the picturesque town of Wetherby is No. 8604, a 1993 Scania N113CRB in service with First Leeds. Wetherby is situated on the River Wharfe along the now bypassed Great North Road. The 1997 Rover on the right-hand side lasted until 2004. Wetherby, June 1999.

The City of Bradford Metropolitan District extends well to the north of the metropolis, taking in Haworth, Keighley, Burley-in-Wharfedale, Ilkley, Menston and Silsden. Close to the Yorkshire Dales National Park is the village of Addingham, where No. 2756 of the Keighley Bus Company was photographed on service 62 to Ilkley. Addingham, November 2021.

Menston railway station was opened in 1865 by the Midland Railway. Trains on this popular commuter line connect either Bradford or Leeds with Ilkley. The link to Otley was regrettably severed in 1965. Transdev's 'Otley Dash' branded service provides a useful link between Menston and Otley. Optare Solo No. 155 was pictured at Menston on 20 November 2021.

Two Wright StreetDecks form an impressive pair at Cleasby Road, Menston, on the Leeds to Otley service on 20 November 2021. On the left is No. 35545 and on the right is No. 35593. Much of Menston has a cosy suburban atmosphere, typical of the rural-urban fringe to the north of Bradford and Leeds.

The striking Transdev 'Dalesway' branding has echoes of the post-deregulation livery of Badgerline, Eastern National and Kentish Bus. No. 2778, a Wright/Volvo B9TL combination, calls in at Steeton bound for Skipton. Although a village, Steeton is the location of the Airedale General Hospital, which serves Keighley, Skipton and parts of the Pendle district in Lancashire. Steeton, March 2022.

One of the smaller mill towns in Bradford district is Silsden, which is situated on both the River Aire and the Leeds and Liverpool Canal. 'Urban Cool' branded No. 1343 is an elderly Volvo B10BLE with Wright Renown bodywork. A testament to Volvo's reliability, it was new in 2000 to Blackburn Transport.

Buses in South and West Yorkshire

25

Laycock is pleasantly situated above Keighley, with fine views of both the town and the often bleak Pennine countryside. Approaching the extremely narrow village centre is 'Keighley Jets' branded Optare Solo No. 152. Some of the houses in Laycock date back to 1685.

Keighley Bus Company No. 1849 is a Wright-bodied Volvo B7RLE, resplendent in this cheerful green livery. It was photographed at Coronation Mount, Braithwaite, on the hilly northern slopes of Keighley.

First's presence in the Keighley area was fairly limited in January 1997. In 'Kingfisher Huddersfield' branding, Dennis Lance/Plaxton Verde No. 4005 had arrived in Keighley on service 502 from Huddersfield. Keighley was placed into Bradford Metropolitan District in 1974 but retains a proud local identity and town council to this day.

Perhaps not the most aesthetically pleasing minibuses, but nevertheless likely to be reliable are the Mellor Strata-bodied Mercedes-Benz Sprinters. New in 2018, No. 51 displays 'Keighley Jets' branding at Aireworth.

No. 1754 in the Keighley Bus Company is a Wright-bodied Volvo B7RLE. With Morton Moor and Riddlesden in the background, No. 1754 was captured high above Keighley at Thwaites Brow during March 2022. Thwaite means 'clearing' or 'reclaimed land' and is a common name in northern England.

Service 662 links Keighley with Bradford through the Aire Valley. Working along the old A650, now the much more tranquil B6265, is Wright-bodied Volvo B7RLE No. 1810, attired in 'The Shuttle' branding. The location is Bradford Road, Riddlesden, during March 2020. East Riddlesden Hall is a popular tourist attraction within Keighley.

Team Pennine operate service 502, an impressive route over the moors linking Keighley with Halifax. Volvo B7RLE No. 1718 makes slow progress through an early morning traffic jam at Denholme during March 2022. No. 1718 previously worked for Transdev's Rosso operation in Rochdale.

No. 2759 is a Wright-bodied B7TL in service with the Keighley Bus Company. Possibly one of the nicest Transdev colour schemes, No. 2759 was snapped entering Bingley on 9 September 2021. Bingley's most famous attraction is Five Rise Locks, which opened in 1774 as part of the Leeds and Liverpool Canal project.

Despite the opening of the controversial Bingley relief road, the town centre still suffers from traffic congestion at peak times. Making slow progress through the centre of Bingley is No. 151 of the Keighley Bus Company. It is an Optare Solo working route K19 to the village of Cullingworth, a few miles above Bingley.

Service 619 connects High Eldwick with Bradford via Harden, Sandy Lane and Allerton. Pictured at the High Eldwick terminus, above Bingley, is 'Pulse' branded No. 37712. The hourly service has duration of approximately sixty-two minutes. Eldwick, March 2022.

Alexander-bodied Scania N113DRB was pictured working one of a number of lengthy services connecting Bradford and Leeds. The 97 was a renumbering of the 655/755 route inherited from West Yorkshire Road Car and Yorkshire Rider. Alternative bus options included the 72 and fast X6 (Huddersfield–Bradford–Leeds). First No. 8023 was pictured in a sylvan setting at Baildon during October 2001.

Saltaire derives its name from Sir Titus Salt, who built a model industrial community on the banks of the River Aire near Shipley. The whole complex is designated a World Heritage Site. Pictured at Bradford Road, Saltaire, is No. 31138, an elderly Volvo B7TL. Note the Covid-19 sign – very much a symbol of the times.

Heaton was long regarded as Bradford's best suburb. Large villas and leafy streets dominate the streets around Lister Park, in what is now pleasant but distinctly inner-city terrain. First No. 37040 turns into Park View Road, past what was Vianney House, bound for Bingley. Photographed on 6 November 2021 at Heaton.

First No. 37713, attired with a poppy, approaches a bus stop at Duckworth Lane, Girlington, on a supremely chilly 6 November 2021. Girlington's population is predominantly South Asian.

Bradford Interchange was opened in March 1977 as a multi-mode and multi-level transport hub. The complex included a railway station, bus concourse, taxi ranks, shops and a large bus depot. Various First Group buses are seen at the Interchange in this June 1998 shot, including Leyland Olympian No. 5140. An Alexander-bodied Scania N113DRB departs for Leeds on the 755 in the distance.

Yorkshire Rider Leyland Olympian/Roe No. 5040 was pictured emerging from the gloom of Bradford Interchange depot during July 1995. The depot lay beneath the bus stops and was also accessible from Nelson Street.

West Yorkshire PTE's last Roe-bodied Leyland Atlanteans featured a revised, slightly blander appearance than earlier designs. In Yorkshire Rider ownership, No. 6325 poses for the camera at Bradford Interchange in 1995, with the destination set for Clayton.

Bradford Traveller's Leyland Atlantean/Roe combination No. 6047 looks in need of thorough clean at Bradford Interchange during February 1997. It carries an unpopular fare box for revenue and advertises an off-peak fare of just 80p. No. 6087 is bound for Allerton, pronounced 'Ol-er-ton', a settlement on the western edge of Bradford (pronounced by some 'Brat-fud').

Keighley & District was formed out of the former West Yorkshire Road Car operations in the north-west of Bradford district. There was no Yorkshire Rider Keighley, as Blazefield purchased the company. Gardner-powered Leyland Olympian No. 363 was working to Oakworth near Keighley on 7 July 1996. Bradford Interchange.

Yorkshire Rider painted several buses in a relatively short-lived 'Flagship' branding. Looking a little grimy and hardly of 'Flagship' quality, an unidentified Leyland Olympian/Roe combination departs Bradford Interchange for Clayton on 9 July 1996.

The neat lines of Northern Counties 'Greater Manchester standards' bodywork is shown to good effect in this photograph of No. 7209 at Bradford Interchange. New to Greater Manchester, this Leyland Fleetline was operating for First Calderline. The Halifax and Huddersfield divisions of West Yorkshire PTE and Yorkshire Rider were keen Fleetline users, Atlanteans predominating in Bradford and Leeds. Taken on 9 July 1996.

Relatively uncommon amongst the large numbers of Yorkshire Rider Atlanteans was the Northern Counties-bodied variant. No. 6423 was new to Greater Manchester PTE in 1978, and came to Yorkshire Rider a decade later. Here it swings into The Tyrls bound for the Buttershaw estate on 9 July 1996.

Bradford Interchange was being reconstructed in 1997. This view shows the remains of stands D and E. A quartet of buses and coaches are seen at rest in May 1997. Bradford Exchange station, renamed Bradford Interchange in 1983, can be seen on the left-hand side. The Interchange was rebuilt again in 2001.

A group of schoolchildren cross The Tyrls, Bradford, during 1998. Alexander-bodied Leyland Olympian No. 5213 waits patiently at a spot now occupied by City Park.

The village of Thornton was the birthplace of the Brontë sisters, but is unfortunately far less popular as a tourist destination than nearby Haworth. Service 607 from Bradford terminates at Thornton Cemetery, high above the city centre. Leaving the terminus on 10 March 2022 is First No. 63277, a nimble Wright StreetLite.

Queensbury was the home of Black Dyke Mills, which has now been converted into business units. Paul McCartney used the Black Dyke Mills Band for the song 'Martha My Dear' in 1968, and again for the Wings 1979 swansong 'Back to the Egg'. First No. 33873 works through a busy Queensbury bound for Halifax in March 2022.

Saltaire and Shipley form the backdrop for First No. 69566 as it makes the steep climb up Carr Lane, Wrose. A Wright-bodied Volvo B7RLE, it was heading to Bradford Interchange on 10 September 2021.

Named *Satnam Singh*, First No. 63280, traverses the large post-war Bradford suburb of Thorpe Edge. Service 671 connects Thorpe Edge with West Bowling.

Double-deckers also serve the Thorpe Edge estate. The distinctive frontal treatment of Wright-bodied Volvo B9TL No. 37090 is shown to good effect at Thorpe Edge on a clammy 9 September 2021.

Almost in Pudsey, First service 687 approaches the Foston Lane terminus at Fagley Road, Bradford, worked by a Wright-bodied Volvo B7RLE new in 2009. A large bakery at Gain Lane, Fagley, usually provides a pleasant aroma around this part of east Bradford. Fagley, March 2022.

Wright StreetLite No. 63278 was new in 2015. Named *Ron Hiley*, it was caught at work on a surprisingly quiet Killinghall Road, Bradford Moor, during September 2021.

At Leeds Old Road, Thornbury, First No. 31790 passes the Woodhall Retail Park en route for Bradford. Other services take the A647, Leeds Road, which descends gradually down to the city centre, amidst endless parked cars and traffic congestion. Thornbury, September 2021.

The pavement on the right-hand side of this photograph, at Dick Lane, is the administrative boundary between Bradford and Leeds. First No. 33885, an Alexander Dennis Enviro400, works service 508 between Leeds and Halifax, a route which avoids the centre of Bradford.

Arriva have a solid presence in the south-east side of Bradford on the routes to Dewsbury and Wakefield. No. 1458, a Wright-bodied VDL SB200, calls at Tong Street, Dudley Hill, on 5 November 2021.

Holme Wood is a large post-war housing estate on the edge of Bradford, featuring mainly low-rise dwellings. Pictured at Stirling Crescent is this fine Volvo B7TL, new in 2004 and still giving adequate service during March 2022.

At Highbridge Terrace, West Bowling, is First No. 63286, another ubiquitous Wright StreetLite. It was working the hourly 671 between West Bowling and Thorpe Edge on a drab 6 November 2021.

Speeding out of New Bank, Halifax, is Enviro400 No. 33888, pursued by Volvo B7RLE No. 66748. They are working a First school service to Lightcliffe Academy along the dramatic A58 road towards Stump Cross. Halifax is the principal town in Calderdale, a district which also includes Brighouse, Elland and Todmorden. September 2021.

Service 576 between Halifax and Bradford is guaranteed to disturb those suffering from vertigo. The stretch between Boothtown and Catherine Slack runs close to the edge of a steep precipice that stands above Ovenden. Working through Boothtown, with Halifax town centre as a backdrop, is First No. 37700, a 2009 Volvo B9TL/Wright combination.

If GM Buses had survived and purchased the Optare Solo, they might have looked something like this. No. 178 operates for Team Pennine and was pictured at Free School Lane, Skircoat, on the Halifax–Ripponden Circular. Halifax, September 2021.

A peek through First's Elmwood depot on a dark and wet teatime on 5 November 2021. Wright-bodied Volvo B9TL No. 37691 shares garage space with an unidentified Enviro400, safe from projectiles and fireworks.

Another angle reveals a trio of Wright-bodied single-deckers and the usual health and safety signage. Elmwood depot is a reasonably long walk from Halifax centre, so be warned if you plan to visit on foot!

The exterior grounds of Elmwood depot show a typical Halifax scene – hills, mills and plenty of verdant green colours. Parked up in the depot yard are a quartet of First buses being used on school services on 9 September 2021, the most interesting being the BMC 220 Condor resplendent in 'myBus' branding.

First No. 32541 was new in February 2005, and is typical of most modern buses in being durable and presentable after years of arduous service. A Wright-bodied Volvo B7TL, which arrived via First Eastern Counties, it was pictured loading at Southgate, Elland, on 3 February 2022. The now cleared Elland Power Station of 1954 was a prominent landmark in the town for several decades.

First No. 37047 climbs up a bitterly cold Sowerby Street, Sowerby Bridge, on 2 December 2021. The town is situated on the River Calder below Halifax amidst steep hills, mills and, rather surprisingly, a few post-war tower blocks.

A failed LDV Convoy owned by Johnsons Coaches of Low Moor causes problems for undergraduates from Trinity and All Saints, Horsforth, in 1999. The minibus was taking the history faculty on a study of Luddenden, a village west of Halifax with numerous notable buildings including Upper Stubbings and Hartley Royd.

Mytholmroyd was the birthplace of the esteemed poet Ted Hughes, whose works include 'The Hawk in the Rain' (1957) and 'Moortown' (1979). Mytholmroyd is situated between Hebden Bridge and Todmorden, and is extremely susceptible to flooding. Photographed near the River Calder is First No. 66710, working towards Halifax.

Rosso No. 2802 is a Transbus Dennis Trident/East Lancs Myllenium Lolyne new to Nottingham City Transport in 2004. At this time East Lancs were using their own unique spelling of words such as millennium, much to the annoyance of lexicographers and English specialists. No. 2802 departs Todmorden for Rawtenstall on a freezing 2 December 2021.

Team Pennine operate service 22 to Claremount via Boothtown. No. 215 is an Optare Versa photographed at Boothtown, with Halifax town centre as a backdrop. Boothtown features the planned industrial village of Akroyden, the brainchild of Colonel Akroyd, who built Hayley Hill Mills in 1836. The elegant spire of All Souls, another Akroyd development, can be seen in the background.

Cleckheaton is situated in the West Yorkshire district of Kirklees. Arriva No. 1978, an ADL Enviro400 departs the modern bus station for Leeds during February 2022. Wright-bodied VDL DB300 No. 1549 is in the background.

Arriva's aquamarine livery is brightened by harsh February sunlight at Bradford Road, Liversedge. No. 1106 is a Volvo B7RLE/Wright Eclipse Urban combination pictured on the 268 to Wakefield. Liversedge was, until 1974, part of a local government district known as Spenborough. Other Spenborough settlements included Birkkenshaw and Cleckheaton, but not Heckmondwike.

Arriva Optare Solo No. 409 leaves Heckmondwike depot amidst a storm of almost biblical intensity, which turned the streets of the Heavy Woollen district into something briefly resembling the film *Waterworld*. Heckmondwike, 9 September 2021.

Another West Yorkshire village associated with the Brontë sisters is Birstall. Charlotte Brontë used Oakwell Hall as the model for 'Fieldhead' in her 1849 novel *Shirley*. At Birstall Market Place, Arriva No. 1103 boards passengers for Leeds during November 2021. In 1937 Birstall merged with nearby Batley, both becoming a part of Kirklees in 1974.

Speeding into a wet Batley bus station, Arriva No. 1051 is an Alexander Dennis Enviro200. Mills are a prominent feature in Batley, a town, from the late 1950s, that attracted a large number of South Asian immigrants to work in the textile industry. For fans of trivia, Roy Orbison met his second wife in Batley.

J. J. Longstaff & Sons once operated a small bus and coach fleet from their base in Mirfield. The bus fleet included everything from a Northern Counties-bodied Leyland Atlantean to a 1996 Dennis Lance. Longstaff ceased trading in 2011 but the name is still used by A. Lyles & Son of Batley. Above Dewsbury, Optare Tempo YJ10MDV completes a school run at Thornhill Edge on 3 February 2022.

Settlements ending in 'thorp' or 'thorpe' are usually of Old Norse or Old English origin. Good examples would include Dogsthorpe, Gunthorpe and Nunthorpe. Ravensthorpe is an exception, being a nineteenth-century creation and an outlier of Dewsbury. With a backdrop of industrial architecture, Arriva No. 1923 works towards Dewsbury from Ravensthorpe on 9 September 2021.

Resplendent in the smart Longstaff livery, Wright Streetlite DF SK63KOB stands at Huddersfield Road, Mirfield, during December 2021. At Battyeford, to the west of Mirfield, is the famous College of the Order of the Resurrection.

Climbing up the steep Woodhouse Hill, Sheepridge, is First No. 69419, a typical Wright-bodied Volvo B7RLE. The suburbs of Huddersfield tend to be hilly, and like Bradford, verdant green hills and bleak moors are never far from sight. Sheepridge, November 2021.

Arriva buses operating in Huddersfield use the busy A62, forerunner of the M62, on routes to Dewsbury and Leeds. In 'Sapphire' branding, Arriva No. 1945 battles heavy traffic at Leeds Road, Bradley, on 9 October 2021.

First Huddersfield's No. 68693 is a BMC Condor resplendent in 'myBus Metro' branding for school services in West Yorkshire. A rare vehicle, it was seen at Keldregate School, Bradley, during November 2021.

The Kingfisher Huddersfield colour scheme bore the closest resemblance to the former Yorkshire Rider livery. Entering Huddersfield's large bus station, opened in 1974, No. 6316, a Leyland Atlantean/Roe combination, looks freshly repainted in the subsidiaries new colour scheme during January 1998.

Contrasting bus designs and liveries at Huddersfield during the fateful month of September 2001. Yorkshire Traction No. 256 is a Leyland National 2, bound for Denby Dale and not 'Denby Dal' as the destination reads. First Huddersfield No. 4041 is a Dennis Lance built in 1995, with distinctive Plaxton Verde bodywork.

Making its way through thick morning traffic is First No. 37687 at Halifax Road, Birchencliffe. This part of Huddersfield is close to junction 24 of the M62, hence the heavy traffic flows. In the 1990s BBC Radio Leeds reported predictions the M62 might eventually come to an entire standstill. Birchencliffe, 5 November 2021.

Team Pennine use the former Yorkshire Traction depot at Waterloo, Huddersfield. Wright-bodied No. 1222, in Yorkshire Tiger livery, appeared to be out of service when photographed in March 2022. Looking healthier is 'Holmfirth Explorer' branded Optare Tempo No. 1406. Transdev purchased Yorkshire Tiger from Arriva in July 2021, renaming the company Team Pennine.

Also parked up at Waterloo depot in March 2022 are two elderly Volvo B7TLs with East Lancs bodywork constructed at Blackburn in 2004. Both carry a 7,300cc engine and have a revenue weight of 17,000 kg. A local urban legend claims you can still hear the ghostly sounds of long departed Yorkshire Traction Leyland Nationals late at night.

Mills dominate the small but pretty town of Slaithwaite. First No. 32461 departs Carr Lane bound for Huddersfield via Linthwaite. Slaithwaite is another Pennine community that is likely to cause outsiders pronunciation issues.

A smart and practical bus for the hilly streets around Golcar is Team Pennine's No. 729. An Alexander Dennis Enviro200, it was working towards Huddersfield, the chief town in Kirklees. Golcar is pronounced 'Gow-kuh'.

Wright-bodied Volvo B7RLE No. 66784 climbs up the steep and narrow Scar Lane, Milnsbridge, during March 2022.

Back in Huddersfield proper, First No. 30949 is an Alexander-bodied Volvo B7TL, pictured on a morning school service at Birkby. The ALX400 body still looks impressive in this November 2021 photograph.

In March 2019, TM Travel of Halfway were operating service 29 using Optare Solo No. 1190. The service connects Holmfirth with Sheffield via Dunford Bridge, Thurgoland and Chapeltown. A scenic service over the South Yorkshire moors, No. 1190 was bereft of customers when this photograph was taken at Holmfirth during a storm in March 2019.

New Mill, not to be confused with New Mills in Derbyshire, stands at a road junction linking the village with Holmfirth, Huddersfield, Barnsley and Sheffield. Team Pennine No. 747 brightens a dull day at Huddersfield Road while on route X1 to Wakefield. New Mill, March 2022.

Front and rear prospects of West Riding Leyland Lynxes at Ossett around 1996. No. 255 displays the distinctive Lynx Mk 1 front with angled driver's windscreen. No. 314 shows off the neat and functional engine compartment, which tended to be less grimy than the Lynxes predecessor, the Leyland National. Ossett bus station was rebuilt in 2005.

The new order at Wakefield in November 1998, following the demise of West Riding. Still in West Riding livery is Optare Metrorider No. 737, while Volvo B10B/Alexander Strider No. 427 carries Arriva's rather drab corporate colours.

A line up of five buses of varying size at Wakefield. Leading is Yorkshire Traction No. 275, a Scania K93CRB/Wright Endurance new in 1992. Behind is an unidentified MCW Metrorider, which appears to be on a Riva Bingo contract. Photographed in September 2001, a month that will be marked by historians, as a turning point in the geopolitical sphere.

Despite Arriva ownership, West Riding No. 528 was still carrying the simplified post-deregulation livery at Castleford in June 1999. Castleford is situated in the Wakefield district of West Yorkshire, with an industrial history based on coal mining, chemicals and glass production. A Roman fort is believed to lay beneath the old bus station.

An early morning photograph at the former West Riding depot at Wheldon Road, Castleford. The Roman name for Castleford was Legiolium. Wheldale Colliery was situated along Wheldon Road. Castleford, March 2022.

Airedale is a large housing estate on the edge of Castleford, within sight of Ferrybridge Power Station. On a bitterly cold November morning, Arriva's VDL SB200/Wright combination No. 1485 collects passengers for the early run to Castleford. Airedale, 20 November 2021.

Pictured at the Old Great North Road, Ferrybridge, Ross Travel's Optare Solo (YJ15 AXS) was struggling to make a safe right turn onto The Square. Heavy traffic and pouring rain made driving hazardous on 11 March 2022.

Arriva No. 1005, an ADL (Alexander Dennis) Enviro200, has just cleared the A1246 flyover, which had been the A1 until the opening of the new A1M to the west of Ferrybridge. A few old structures survive in the town amidst the modern buildings, the most notable being the Old Bridge of 1797, which links Ferrybridge with Brotherton in North Yorkshire, and is now restricted to pedestrians.

The reconstructed Ferrybridge Power Station dominates Arriva No. 1897 as it heads towards Knottingley. Power Stations A, B and C were decommissioned in 1976, 1992 and 2016 respectively, with Multifuel plants 1 and 2 coming into operation between 2015 and 2019. Construction of Ferrybridge D power station is expected to commence around 2025. Knottingley, 20 November 2021.

Heath Hall and Heath Common provide a beautiful oasis just a few miles from Wakefield. Arriva's Wright-bodied VDL SB200 passes John Carr's Heath Hall (1754) at Kirkthorpe Lane. The once dominant Wakefield Power Station has been demolished but the views of Wakefield Cathedral are obscured by towers in the city centre. Heath, March 2022.

Close to the site of the now cleared Goosehill Junction is the village of Warmfield. Approaching the settlement from Kirkthorpe is Arriva No. 1472, working service 186 to Pontefract during March 2022.

CT Plus was operating Wright-bodied Volvo B7TL No. 1988, on the St Wilfrid's School (Featherstone) service in March 2022. Running almost empty, it was pictured amidst modern street clutter at Normanton.

Yorkshire Traction always operated a diverse and interesting fleet. Notable bus types have included low-height MCW Metrobuses and the unusual Spartan chassis constructed in the United States. No. 290, a Northern Counties-bodied Scania L113CRL, was photographed at Pontefract in June 1999. The hapless Richard II was probably murdered in Pontefract Castle in 1400.

Featherstone is situated between Wakefield and Pontefract, part of West Yorkshire's former colliery country. The Featherstone massacre of 1893 witnessed the shooting of at least two miners during a national lockout, and a memorial stands in the town centre to remember the tragedy. Optare Solo YJ18 CZY was being operated by Ross Travel on service 146 at dusk on 18 November 2021.

Yorkshire Traction No. 425 is a Wright-bodied Dennis Dart working service 245 to Barnsley. The Dart was a tremendous success for Dennis being exactly the right bus, at the right time, compared to the relatively unsuccessful Lancet and Falcon range. Hemsworth, 1999.

Grimethorpe, a village to the north of Barnsley, suffered badly during the pit closures of the post-war period. The mine closed in May 1993 and new roads and the Park Springs Industrial Estate have been constructed to boost the local economy. Working into Grimethorpe is Stagecoach No. 37088, a typical ADL Enviro200 based at Rawmarsh.

In Yorkshire Traction days Barnsley bus station was a hive of activity. A cacophony of reversing horns and engine sounds, plus thick exhaust smoke, made it a popular place for bus enthusiasts. Now completely rebuilt and known as Barnsley Interchange, the facility is dominated by Stagecoach since the demise of 'the Tracky'. On 10 September 2021 a plethora of mainly Stagecoach buses dominate the scene at Barnsley Interchange.

A trio of Stagecoach buses at Barnsley led by No. 28671, a Scania K230UB with Enviro300 bodywork.

Attired in 'Stagecoach Gold' branding is Chesterfield's No. 11120, an Alexander Dennis Enviro400 at Barnsley. It was working the flagship X17 service to Sheffield and Chesterfield, Derbyshire. Considerable parts of Barnsley were under reconstruction when this photograph was taken in September 2021. The post-war Metropolitan Centre, markets and bus station have now been demolished.

Wombwell is typical of many of the smaller South Yorkshire towns in managing to retain a sense of individuality and independence from the large metropolitan borough it is governed by. R&S Waterson of Badsworth were using MV58 FMY, an ADL Enviro200, on the Wombwell–Doncaster service on 18 November 2021. For the unwary, Wombwell is pronounced 'Wum-wel'.

Representing modern fleet standardisation is Stagecoach No. 22642, at Goldthorpe. An Enviro300, it is constructed on a MAN 18.240 chassis.

Deep in what had been Yorkshire Traction territory, Stagecoach Alexander Dennis Enviro200 No. 37104 works towards Barnsley on the Dearne Valley route at Thurnscoe, 19 November 2021. Other Dearne Valley settlements include Brampton Bierlow, Darfield, Swinton and Wombwell. The source of the River Dearne can be found at Birdsedge, near Denby Dale.

Working through the village of Oxspring in the Pennine area of Barnsley district is YX71 OHV, an Alexander Dennis Enviro200. Service 23 is operated by Globe Holidays (Barnsley) and was on diversion at Oxspring and Thurgoland due to a landslip. Oxspring, March 2022.

Only just in the South Yorkshire district of Doncaster, Bawtry is a pretty but workaday town on the boundary with the Bassetlaw area of Nottinghamshire. The busy High Street thunders with juggernauts heading to East Retford, Gainsborough, Newark, and elsewhere. In heavy traffic, Stagecoach East Midlands No. 34848 heads north towards Doncaster from Gainsborough, Lincolnshire. The bus, new in 2006, is a Dennis Dart with Alexander Pointer 2 bodywork.

Stagecoach Enviro400 No. 10666 is pictured loading for Doncaster at Bawtry. At the rear, No. 35150, an Alexander-Dennis Dart, departs for Misson, a village over the border in Nottinghamshire. Bawtry, March 2022.

Historic Tickhill is a desirable village between Maltby and Bawtry. Little remains of the famous castle, but there is the beautiful St Mary's Church to explore and plenty of pretty streets. Boarding passengers at the Market Cross of 1777 is First No. 37110, in 'Doncaster's Red Buses' branding.

Finningley was transferred from Nottinghamshire to the then new South Yorkshire Metropolitan County in 1974. Now part of Doncaster, the village was once home to the much respected independent bus operator Leon. Today, Robin Hood Airport (Doncaster Sheffield) dominates the site once occupied by RAF Finningley and Leon, have ceased trading. First No. 63137 pauses at The Green, Finningley, in March 2022.

Doncaster was once the Roman town of Danum, standing aside the River Don. Horse racing came around 1700 and later the railways, both giving Doncaster fame around the UK. At St James's Bridge, First No. 69222 heads towards Hexthorpe with bleak post-war housing dominating the background. Taken on 3 December 2021.

Hexthorpe was built as a residential area for workers of 'the Plant', the Doncaster Railway Works. The *Flying Scotsman* and *Mallard* were constructed at 'the Plant', which was opened by the Great Northern Railway in 1853, locomotive production beginning in 1867. First No. 69222 continues its journey along Urban Road, Hexthorpe, amidst rush-hour traffic and parked cars in December 2021.

At Balby, a DAF Wrecker has come to the aid of First Doncaster No. 37234. Even Volvo's breakdown sometimes, but not as much as AEC Merlins and Daimler Roadliners.

Framed by the columns of a road sign showing directions to Rotherham, First No. 36254 works the busy X78 to Sheffield at Warmsworth. An Optare Solo in service with Powells brings up the rear, on the hourly service 18 from Doncaster to Hellaby. The Warmsworth area has a number of dolomite quarries and disused kilns close to the banks of the River Don. Taken at High Road, Warmsworth, on 4 February 2022.

New Edlington is a former colliery village, now generally known as plain Edlington. The pit known as Yorkshire Main Colliery opened in 1909 and was regrettably closed in 1985, despite returning a profit. A sombre winding wheel commemorates the site of the pit. First No. 63125 traverses Edlington Lane on an unsettled 4 February 2022.

The Mexborough and Swinton Traction Company ceased trading in 1969 when it was absorbed by Yorkshire Traction. The 'Tracky' were taken over by Stagecoach in 2005. At Mexborough, Stagecoach No. 36990 loads passengers for Rotherham on 10 September 2021.

Conisborough is a town of considerable interest and antiquity located in a deep cut on the River Don. The former mining town is dominated by Conisborough Castle, built by the de Warenne's around 1180. With a backdrop of the 90-foot castle keep, Stagecoach No. 26031 works out to Doncaster in blazing sunshine. Conisborough, 19 November 2021.

The north-east corner of Doncaster Metropolitan District is a mixture of former colliery villages and more traditional market towns such as Thorne. The flat landscape feels closer in spirit to the neighbouring East Riding and Lincolnshire. The old market town of Thorne is the location of First No. 63143, photographed at Kirton Lane on 4 February 2022.

Passing near the site of Hatfield Main Colliery, which sadly closed in 2015, is First No. 47486 at Station Road, Stainforth. Part of the winding gear was still visible when this picture was taken in February 2022. Also out of view is Hatfield & Stainforth railway station, which provides links to Doncaster, Goole, Hull and Scunthorpe.

A new Ford Puma overtakes First No. 37104 at Station Road, Dunscroft. It is working service 87a to Doncaster. The area around Hatfield was once a hive of independent bus operators including Premier of Stainforth, who operated an Ailsa B55-10 purchased new in 1976.

The magnificent tower of St Lawrence's Church at Hatfield forms the backdrop for 'Doncaster's Red Buses' No. 36237. The livery is reminiscent of the old Doncaster Corporation colours used before the formation of South Yorkshire PTE. Wright-bodied Volvo B9TL was working towards Stainforth on 11 March 2022.

Arriva No. 0664 is a rare MCV Evolution caught on camera at High Street, Bentley. A former mining community to the north of Doncaster, Bentley Colliery was sadly closed in December 1993, leaving the site a wasteland for years. Bentley, November 2021.

A cold night out at Adwick-le-Street. First No. 37103 has just collected passengers at Woodlands on the Great North Road for Doncaster. Woodlands, was built as a model estate for the miners of the now closed Brodsworth Main Colliery. The manuscripts of the priest Robert Parkyn of Adwick-le-Street have been studied by historians such as A. G. Dickens to study Catholic devotion on the eve of the Reformation.

The countryside north of Doncaster, while not spectacular, is certainly pretty. Former colliery villages with ancient foundations are located close to settlements untouched by the Industrial Revolution. Heading towards leafy Burghwallis, First No. 63136 was pictured leaving the expanded village of Campsall, in the parish of Norton, during March 2022.

A sharp left turn on the southbound A1 (Great North Road) leads to the South Yorkshire village of Skellow. Working out to Doncaster, First No. 37103 traverses the leafy surroundings of Crabtree Lane. The writer and hermit Richard Rolle ended his days at a Cistercian nunnery at nearby Hampole in 1349. *Incendium Amoris* is probably his best-known work. Skellow, 19 November 2021.

Contiguous with Skellow, Carcroft has a distinctly post-industrial character. Bullcroft Colliery operated between 1912 and 1970 before merging with the long closed Brodsworth Colliery at Adwick-le-Street. Skellow Road sees Wright-bodied No. 36277 collect passengers for all stops to Doncaster on 11 March 2022.

Leaving the gloomy surroundings of Rotherham Interchange is First No. 35134, attired in 'Steel Link' branding. The Interchange has been significantly refurbished but remains an ungainly example of post-war architecture. Cooling towers once dominated the site giving an oppressive atmosphere to this part of Rotherham.

A stylish but slightly fragile-looking PSV is Powell's Bus P3 WTL. New to Reading, it is a Scania N230UD/East Lancs combination pictured entering Rotherham Interchange in December 2021. The River Don flows next to the bus station underneath Centenary Way.

Powell's Bus (sometimes written Powells Bus) Scania P3 WTL passes the firm's Optare Solo YJ55 BJO at Rotherham on 3 December 2021. Historic structures in Rotherham include All Saints and Bridge Chapel.

First No. 37529 (1529) was photographed at Barbot Hall Industrial Estate, Rotherham, on 10 September 2021. It carries the colours of First's antecedent, SYT (South Yorkshire's Transport). SYT, which later became Mainline, was the successor to South Yorkshire PTE, which had been formed from the Doncaster, Rotherham and Sheffield transport undertakings in 1974.

Near the Don Bridge, First No. 36264 traverses Rawmarsh Road, Rotherham, from Parkgate. A considerable swathe of north Rotherham has been redeveloped with retail facilities such as the Parkgate Shopping Park, replacing heavy industry.

With a backdrop of Rotherham's urban centre, First No. 69512 was pictured on an early morning run to Sheffield at Coronation Bridge, Masbrough. Out of shot is the old Rotherham United Football Ground. Beeversleigh Flats at Clifton form the distinctive tower in the background.

Another early morning shot from Rotherham showing No. 37234, a Wright-bodied Volvo B9TL, in service with First Doncaster at Meadow Bank Road, Jordan. Out of shot are the massive Blackburn Meadows Sewage Works, Templeborough and the possible site of the Battle of Brunanburh (AD 937). Jordan, September 2021.

First No. 63140, a Wright StreetLite, negotiates parked cars and advises passengers to wear a face mask at Kimberworth Park on 18 November 2021. I can confidently confirm this bus is not carrying a personalised plate for the Department of Work and Pensions (DWP).

A cursory glance around the centre of Greasbrough betrays its old village roots. Situated on hilly ground close to the busy retail and industrial units at Parkgate and the steel works at Aldwarke, Greasbrough, was incorporated into Rotherham County Borough in 1936. First No. 33870 stands at Church Street, Greasbrough, during September 2021.

Passing through Thorpe Hesley is First No. 69464, a Wright Eclipse-bodied Volvo B7RLE. The village is close to the peaceful surroundings of Wentworth Woodhouse. Off Scholes Lane is the distinctive landmark known as Keppel's Column, a 115-foot-high Tuscan lookout column built for Wentworth Woodhouse by John Carr in 1778.

The Stagecoach depot at Rawmarsh was acquired as part of the Yorkshire Traction takeover in December 2005. Several training buses were operating around Rawmarsh and Greasbrough on 4 February 2022. No. 22086, an Alexander-bodied MAN 18.220, was doing several circuits of the depot when pictured.

After several circuits, No. 22086 prepares to enter Dale Road, Rawmarsh. Prior to incorporation into Rotherham in 1974, Rawmarsh was an independent urban district above the steel works at Parkgate and Aldwarke.

There are usually one or two buses awaiting a crew change at Rawmarsh depot. On 4 February 2022, Enviro300 No. 37103 rests at the Dale Road bus stop. No. 37089, in the latest livery, prepares to pass, bound for Parkgate and Rotherham.

Wath-upon-Dearne was once dominated by Manvers Main Colliery, Wath Marshalling Yard and numerous slurry lagoons and tips. In the neat town centre, Stagecoach No. 26023 was photographed at the small bus station. The former colliery and coking plants have been dramatically transformed by landscaping, new business parks and housing. Wath-upon-Dearne, 19 November 2021.

With Dalton in the background and the Liberty Special Steel plant out of shot on the right, First No. 37236 is captured at Doncaster Road, Whinney Hill. A short distance away the splendidly named Mushroom Roundabout, and Thrybergh Academy and Foljamba Primary.

First No. 1230 carries Doncaster Corporation heritage livery at Doncaster Road, Thrybergh. The village to the east of Rotherham has some interesting buildings including the partly Norman church of St Leonard and Thrybergh Park, once a country house but now home of Rotherham Golf Club. The nearby Silverwood Colliery closed in 1994.

First Doncaster's Wright-bodied Volvo B9TL works its way up the steep A630 at Hooton Roberts during March 2022. Despite the rural ambience and the prettiness of Hooton Roberts, the industrial Aldwarke, Rotherham and Mexborough are just a few miles away.

In 'Steel Link' branding, First No. 35128, a Wright StreetDeck, works the flagship X1 route from Maltby to Rotherham and Sheffield via Meadowhall. Maltby Colliery survived until March 2013.

One of the older Stagecoach double-deckers in service during December 2021 was No. 18054, a TransBus Trident/TransBus President combination new in 2003. It carries 'Donna the Doncaster Belle' branding at Green Arbour Road, Thurcroft, on 3 December 2021.

Buses in South and West Yorkshire 91

The driver of First No. 37523 has a vape as shoppers emerge from the market at Dinnington on 3 December 2021. Located in Rotherham district, Dinnington was hard hit by the closure of local steel mills and coal mines in the 1980s. Dinnington Colliery closed in 1992.

Plaxton Coach Sales Centre is based at South Anston, within easy reach of the M1 and M18. Photographed in the yard and nearest to the camera is YX69 NXL, an Enviro400 EV demonstrator in London red. On the right is a Transdev 'Rochdale Runners' branded ADL Enviro200.

There were few Stagecoach buses to be seen in South Yorkshire on 3 December 2021 due to a strike. Scania N230UD/Alexander Dennis Enviro400 No. 15717 had made it out and was seen at Deepcar, near Stocksbridge.

Stagecoach buses grace the streets of Sheffield following the takeover of Yorkshire Traction's subsidiaries, which included Sheffield Omnibus and Yorkshire Terrier. In the depot yard at Ecclesfield, various Stagecoach buses are on view after a heavy shower in February 2022.

Also photographed at Ecclesfield, this time in November 2021, is Wright StreetDeck No. 39104. It carries the latest and perhaps most attractive Stagecoach corporate livery.

Firth Park is an extremely diverse neighbourhood of Sheffield. Wright StreetDeck No. 35314 was setting down passengers around Firth Park Road and Stubbin Lane during November 2021. Famous people associated with Sheffield include Joe Cocker, Patrick McGoohan and Mary, Queen of Scots.

Sheffield has been described as a 'dirty picture in a beautiful frame'. The Don Valley has been cleaned up and much of the city centre has undergone regeneration. A trio of First buses including double-deckers Nos 37263 and 37485 are seen at the post-war development of Arundel Gate on 3 December 2021.

TM Travels Optare Versa No. 1197 is blocked by First Alexander Dennis Enviro200 No. 67143, near Castle Square, Sheffield, on a distinctly grimy 3 December 2021. In the aftermath of deregulation, Sheffield had been one of the most competitive centres of bus operation in the UK.

Rows of chimney pots and terrace housing are characteristic of inner-city Sheffield. At Main Road, Darnall First No. 36276, a Wright-bodied Volvo B9TL, works service 52A to Wisewood. Despite Sheffield's image as a city of industry, a significant portion of the district is rural and includes wards within the Peak District National Park.

On the eastern fringe of Sheffield is Woodhouse, located close to the site of Orgreave Works. Ninety-five people were arrested during the notorious Battle of Orgreave between pickets and police on 18 June 1984. Another more ancient battle thought to have taken place in this area was the Battle of Brunanburh (AD 937) at Brinsworth, though some claim Barnsdale, Brombrough, Lanchester et al. First No. 37476 was pictured at Cross Street, Woodhouse, during November 2021.

Sheffield is said to be England's hilliest city and many bus routes have to negotiate steep inclines. The spectacular Gleadless Valley was developed as a series of housing estates from 1955. Houses, maisonettes and high-rise blocks comprise the bulk of the districts housing. Climbing Leighton Road with Sheffield city centre in the background is First No. 37515.

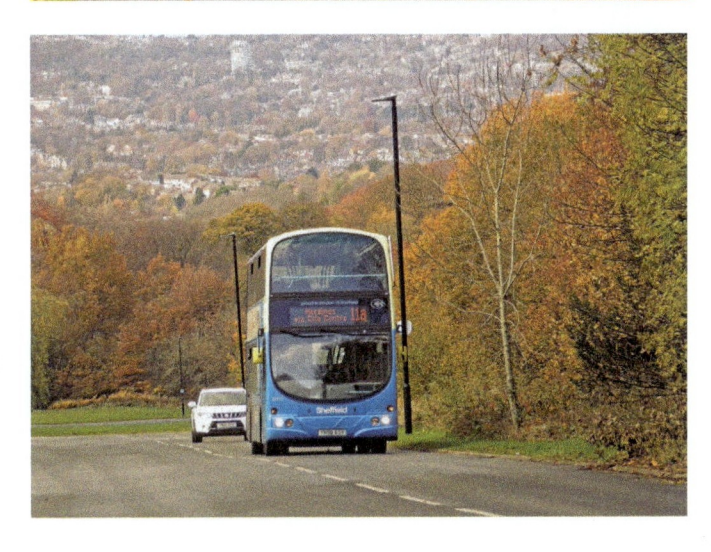

The Gleadless Valley is comprised of various neighbourhoods including Hemsworth, Herdings and Rollestone. The first estate to be constructed was Herdings, where we see First No. 37511, a Wright-bodied Volvo B9TL, on 18 November 2021. The First Sheffield depot is located at Olive Grove.

Sheffield has numerous interesting building designs including the Park Hill development (1956–61). There are also considerable swathes of moorland, much of it located within the Peak District National Park. First No. 63907 was photographed high up at Raeburn Road, Herdings, close to the Derbyshire boundary.

The Sheffield Supertram operated by Stagecoach has served the South Yorkshire city since 1994. There are four routes, namely Yellow, Blue, Purple and Train Tram (TT), operating around Sheffield. Service TT connects Sheffield Cathedral with Rotherham Parkgate. At Malin Bridge, Siemens Duewag No. 119 prepares for a journey to Halfway, a part of Sheffield previously in Derbyshire.